Directions For Breeding Game Cocks
Including Rules and Orders In Old English Cock Fighting

by J. Barker

with an introduction by Jackson Chambers

Self Reliance Books

Get more historic titles on animal and stock breeding, gardening and old fashioned skills by visiting us at:

http://selfreliancebooks.blogspot.com/

Disclaimer

This book was written in an age when cock-fighting was widely acceptable throughout society. In many places throughout the world, cock-fighting has been made illegal.

The material presented herein is intended to be strictly for educational purposes with the purpose of enlightening Game Fowl breeders about the history of their breed. Publication of the material is neither an endorsement, nor a criticism of its contents. This book is presented as part of large series of educational material on the history and raising of numerous chicken breeds for utility or exhibition purposes.

As the reader, please consider it your duty to become familiar with local, state, provincial and federal laws relating to the subject matter contained herein before attempting to utilize any of the information presented.

As the author, publisher and retailer cannot control how the reader utilizes the historical information presented in the pages herein, they hereby disclaim any liability to any party for any loss, damage, disruption or other liability that may be incurred by the reader's misuse of this material.

Introduction

I am pleased to present this third title in the "Game Fowl" series.

This volume is entitled "Directions or Breeding Game Cocks" and was published in 1804.

The work is in the Public Domain and is re-printed here in accordance with Federal Laws.

Though this work is a century old it contains much information on poultry that is still pertinent today.

As with all reprinted books of this age that are intended to perfectly reproduce the original edition, considerable pains and effort had to be undertaken to correct fading and sometimes outright damage to existing proofs of this title. At times, this task is quite monumental, requiring an almost total "rebuilding" of some pages from digital proofs of multiple copies. Despite this, imperfections still sometimes exist in the final proof and may detract from the visual appearance of the text.

I hope you enjoy reading this book as much as I enjoyed making it available to readers again.

Jackson Chambers

DIRECTIONS

FOR

BREEDING GAME COCKS.

MANY gentlemen who follow the diverfion of fighting cocks, by not being well acquainted with the methods concerning breeding them, are prevented from enjoying the moft defirable part of the fancy; therefore, the refult of many yeats experience upon that fubject, I humbly hope, will be well received by all lovers of the fport, or any other perfons who have the curiofity to read the following pages.

The choice of a cock fhould be from a ftrain which has behaved well, that is, from thofe who have always won the odd battle when equally matched; for it is a general opinion among perfons who are well acquainted with the fancy, that cocks capable of fo doing are good ones. I have known perfons who abfolutely have been out of humour with their fort, and parted with them, becaufe they did not all win, without reflecting on the probability there was of other gentlemen having as good cocks as themselves, and who placed as much dependance on them. I have known some people who have only bred a few just to fight for a dinner, change their breed by reason of a cock's losing his second battle; not considering the hurt he might have received in his first, nor the great odds there are against any cock winning twice. For instance, I have seen cocks, that to all appearances won the first time they fought very easy, yet have been very much hurt, and in their second battle, after a few blows, stood still and been beat. Neither is this the only thing against a cock's winning twice; for after having fought the battle he was matched for, it seldom happens but he is neglected; yet an opportunity offering to fight him in the course of eight or ten days, he receives a hurry with another cock in the pens, and because his goodness makes him spar well for some two or three minutes, it is concluded he is fit to fight; and if he has to combat with a cock that has never fought, and well to fight, it is almost certain he will be beat, though perhaps a much better cock in blood.

It sometimes happens during the course of a battle, particularly if one of the cocks is blinded, that the setter to gets a blow in the hand, which will prevent him ufing it for three or four days; judge then what a fituation one of thefe poor animals muft be in from the number of wounds he muft confequently receive during a fmart battle of fifteen or twenty minutes; yet, if a good cock in blood, he will appear in two or three weeks time as if he had not been hurt: but never truft to appearances of this fort, for be affured, after a cock has fought a hard battle, he will not be fit to fight again the fame feafon; and very often, after you have been at the expence and trouble of keeping him at his walk another year, he will only lofe your money, by reafon of his having received fome hurt in his firft battle, which he has never been able to get the better of, and which the beft judge could not difcover.

I remember a circumftance of this kind happening to a neighbouring gentleman, who having entered into an agreement to fight a week's play, at a very fhort notice, and not being able to get a fufficient number of cocks he could depend upon, had the temerity to weigh in fome of his own ftags, of about ten or eleven months old, and it fo happened that one of them had to fight againft the cock the other party depended moft upon winning; but after a doubtful and bloody conteft for near half an hour, contrary to the opinion of every one prefent, the ftag came off victorious, which fo elated his mafter, that he fent him to one of his beft walks to run till the next feafon; but what was very extraordinary, he moulted from a dark red to a very light ginger pile. This ftrange metamorphofe we were totally at a lofs to account for, when we were informed by a perfon who fpoke pertinently upon the fubject, that it was owing to his having been fo feverely handled in his battle, that he had feen two or three inftances of the fame kind; and at the fame time advifed my friend never to fight him again, for it was almoft reduced to a certainty that he would be beat if he happened to fall in weight with a good cock. But this piece of advice my friend did not attend to, having him weighed in the very next match he made, and in which he met with the fate his mafter had been fore-warned of (making hardly any defence), although as well to fight, with regard to the feeding part, as it was poffible for a cock to be.

But lofing the battle money, and betts to a confiderable amount, were not the only loffes my friend met with on this occafion, for he had turned down four of his beft hens to him, fo that he loft a whole feafon from them, befides the expence of bringing up between twenty and thirty chickens, until they were near eight months old, whofe necks I think he acted very wifely in breaking, not choofing to truft to that expreffion fo often made ufe of by inexperienced fanciers, " They may be good."

It is probable this mode of reafoning may be objected to, particularly by fome who have been fortunate enough to have bred good chickens from a cock that has fought feveral times; alfo by thofe who have had cocks that have won feveral hattles. Yet, I have known cocks that have fought feveral times get good chickens, but then they have had an elegance of make, and a remarkable found conftitution, to recommend them; and indeed, if they had not been poffeffed of fomething very rare to be found in the common run of cocks, I am fure a perfon of judgment would never have bred from them. As to cocks winning feveral battles, I muft own that it fometimes happens that a cock will win three or four feafons running in regular matches, or win a Welch main *,

---

* A Welch main is when fixteen cocks, which muft not exceed a certain weight, are to fight for a prize; and the method to match them is, when they are weighed, to fee that none of them exceeds the weight fpecified; thofe that fall neareft each other fight, which confequently makes eight battles: then the eight winners fight again, which makes four battles; and the four winners, two battles; and the two winners, one battle. So that one cock is obliged to win four times to come off victorious; and the fame method with regard to matching thofe that are neareft in weight, is obferved every time they fight.

but then he muſt be a very ſevere ſtriker; and
for another's winning ſeven or eight battles in a
ſeaſon, it ought to be conſidered what he has
had to fight againſt, a parcel of half bred, ill-
walked, dung-hill things; or elſe ſome young
fanciers have been prevailed upon to fight chickens againſt him, or cocks much under his
weight; when if he had had a freſh cock come
againſt him only the ſecond time he fought, of
equal weight and goodneſs, and as well to
fight, it is very great odds but he muſt have
been beat.

After this digreſſion, let us return to deſcribe
the properties a cock ought to be poſſeſſed of
that is bred from; and having before remarked
that you ſhould be well acquainted with the
ſtock he ſprung from, the next object you muſt
pay an attention to, is to be aſſured he is perfectly ſound, which to find out is rather diffi-
cult; but the beſt method I can adviſe is
ſtrictly to obſerve his manner of feeding, for if
he will eat corn enough to make his crop very
hard, and digeſt it quickly, it is a ſure ſign his
conſtitution is good, as it is that he is rotten,
if he eats but little, and has a bad digeſtion.

There are alſo other methods to be obſerved
on this occaſion, ſuch as running him down in
a field, or to ſpar him with another cock,

when if he turns black in the face, at either of thefe exercifes, you may be certain he is not found; but to make fure, try thefe, and every other method you can devife; for it is impoffible to be too particular in this article.

As to the exterior qualifications, his head fhould be thin and long, or if fhort, very taper, with a large full eye, his beak crooked and ftout, his neck thick and long, (for a cock with a long neck has a great advantage in his battle, particularly if his antagonift is one of thofe kind of cocks that will fight at no other place but the head); his body fhort and compact, with a round breaft (as a fharp breafted cock carries a great deal of ufelefs weight about him, and never has a fine fore-hand); his thighs firm and thick, and placed well up to the fhoulder (for when a cock's thighs hang dangling behind him, be affured he never can maintain a long battle); his legs long and thick, and if they correfpond with the colour of his beak, I think it a perfection; and his feet fhould be broad and thin, with very long claws.

With regard to his carriage, he fhould be upright, but not ftiffly fo; his walk fhould be ftately, with his wings in fome meafure extended, and not plod along as I have feen fome cocks do, with their wings upon their backs like geese.

As to the colour he is of, I think it immaterial, for there are good cocks of all colours; but he should be thin of feathers, and they short and very hard, which is another proof of his being healthy; as on the contrary, if he has many, and those soft and long, it favours much of his having a bad constitution.

A cock possessed of all these qualifications, supposing him in a condition to fight, ought not to weigh more than four pounds eight or ten ounces; for if you breed from a cock that weighs five pounds and upwards, and your hens are of a good size, which they ought to be, the cocks they produce, if well walked, will be too large to fight within the articles, and this will be a great loss to the breeder; neither should they weigh much less than the weight I have mentioned, for if he is not greatly superior in size to the hens you put him with, the produce will not have that share of bone they should have, and consequently if they fight against well bred cocks, they will lose a great deal in match, which every one that follows this fancy knows the result of, or at least should do.

Having mentioned the requisites for the choice of a cock, be certain the hens you intend him to breed with are found; which to find out, use the same methods that I have mentioned to be made use of with a cock; also be assured there has not been the least taint in their race for many generations past. As to other qualifications with regard to feather, make, and shape, they should exactly correspond with the cock's, except their bodies, which should be roomy behind, for the production of large eggs.

The next thing to be considered is the place for you to breed at; this should at least be near half a mile from any house where fowls are kept, for fear of having your hens trod by other cocks, which is often the case if they ramble within sight of each other: likewise it should be a considerable distance from any wood or coppice; that is, it ought to be so far, that there would not be a probability of their straying near it, for the vermin that infest those places will destroy your chickens; and sometimes it affords an opportunity for a fox to run away with your cock, or one of your hens during the day time.

If your situation is on a dry gravelly soil, it is the better, and as you must by no means breed at a place where there is not a constant spring of clear water, contrive if you can to let it run off in a small stream by the house, if ever so inconsiderable; by which means your fowls will always have clean water without any trouble; but if you are obliged to draw the water out of your well with a bucket, be attentive to give it them fresh very often.

It is the prevailing opinion among many persons, who are fanciers, that a farm house is a good place to breed game chickens, because of the many out-houses and stables for them to take shelter in during bad weather; and thinking as they are threshing the greatest part of the year, there will be always food for them. It is true, dry places where they may amuse themselves when it rains are very convenient, but buying them corn should be of no moment to a gentleman who wishes to see his cocks cut a figure in a match.

As it is probable the Reader would wish to know my objections against breeding at a farm-house; they are because people in general keep a number of hogs, geese, and ducks, which foul all the water about the place, and unless chickens have clean water, they will never make thorough sound cocks. Neither do I think it a good walk for a cock, on account of the many hens that are ufually kept at thefe places; for it muft be underftood, by his having fo great a variety he will debilitate himfelf; and to clear up this point, is only determining whether a debilitated perfon is able to go through the fame exercifes as one who has never entered into any debaucheries. Alfo, as I have obferved already concerning the water, it is abfolutely as neceffary that cocks and hens fhould have clean water, as well as chickens, if you mean to keep them found *. But to finifh the defcription of the fituation you fhould choofe to breed at, let the place where they are to rooft in be dry, and free from any offenfive fmells; as to the fize of it, it is not very material, only do not let it be too fmall, nor the roofting perch too thick for them to gripe, nor higher than they can afcend and defcend with eafe; which will prevent them from having fwelled feet, a defect that fhould be carefully guarded againft, it being looked upon fo detrimental, that feeders have refufed to accept them, when they have been perfect in

* I do not mean to deter people from eating fowls when I fay they are not found, for they really eat the better for it, and which may eafily be known by killing two chickens of the fame age, letting one be thriving and hardy, and the other rather weakly. Now permit them both to be dreffed exactly alike, and when they are brought to table, the thriving chicken will look black and eat hard, the other tender, and appear delicately white.

every other respect; which consequently must be a great loss to those who only breed cocks to lend.

In the beginning of February put your cock and hens together, and not before, taking care that your hens have not been with any cock since they laid their last clutch of eggs; also regulate the number you put down according to the quantity of chickens you want to breed, but never put more than four to one cock, and let them be sisters, for by putting different sorts together, you never can breed with any certainty: likewise, I think it necessary you should pay an attention to how they agree, for if the cock takes a dislike to any one of the hens (as it is sometimes the case), take her up, for you had better lose breeding with her a season, than to have chickens when there is the least probability of their turning out badly.

Before your hens begin to lay, provide separate nests for them, for if there is only one, and as they generally want to lay about the same time in the day, it will occasion them to drop their eggs in improper places, and sometimes to quarrel: likewise, let them be as far asunder as the breeding place will admit of.

The firſt egg they lay, as it generally runs a great deal ſmaller than the reſt of the clutch, I would not have you ſave, but let it be marked and left for a neſt egg; this done, take all the others out of the neſt the ſame day they are laid, and put them in a box with bran, taking care they are not thrown about nor changed; for ſome perſons who breed cocks think it no harm to get poſſeſſion of another's ſtrain (no matter by what means), if they believe they are better than their own; but to be certain if this happens, write your name upon every egg you mean to ſet, directly as you take it out of the neſt, which is the hardeſt mark to counterfeit, and which, though your eggs may be ſtolen, will prevent your being deceived.

When your hens begin to grow broody, do not ſave any more of their eggs, but leave them in the neſt, as it will entice them to ſit the ſooner; and my reaſon for your acting in this manner, is, that after they ſhew a deſire of wanting to ſit, they are never in perfect health, which may be perceived by their countenance turning white, the ſhrivelling of their combs, and by their ſcreaming when the cock comes near them; nor will they ever permit him to tread them but when he does it by ſurpriſe; therefore, it is not likely the chickens thoſe eggs produce, could poſſeſs the ſpirit that chickens produced from eggs laid by the hens when they are in full health; and it is really my opinion, this is the reason why two forts of chickens (fome very good ones, and others but indifferent) have been hatched at the fame time from the produce of one cock and hen; and if it has happened that the eggs laid while fhe was in health have been deftroyed during the time of fitting, and thofe laid by her after fhe began to grow broody preferved, the hen or cock, or perhaps both, have had their necks broke for breeding bad chickens, when at the fame time, it has not been their demerit, but the perfon whofe care they were entrufted to.

Having made thefe remarks with regard to the eggs the moft proper to fit on, it is probable you will want to have two clutches of chickens from each of your hens; in a proper feafon to effect which, do not let them fit upon the firft clutch of eggs they lay, but provide hens for that purpofe, whether dunghill or game is not very material, but I think the former is to be preferred, as by their being lefs apt to quarrel, the chickens will not run fo much danger of being trod to death; but make yourfelf thoroughly affured they have not got that fatal diftemper called the roope.

When you fet them, let their nefts be made in large earthen pans, at leaft a foot and a half from the ground, with clean ftraw rubbed foft, which will prevent their being annoyed by vermin, for I have known hens actually killed by fwarms of fmall infects that have found means to get at them when they have been fet in old boxes or tubs; which accidents pans will entirely prevent. As to the number of eggs you put under each hen, they ought not to exceed twelve; for a hen feldom hatches more than that number of chickens if fhe fit upon feventeen, by reafon of her not being able to give them all the proper degree of heat they require; and very often by having fo many, fpoils them all; neither do I think it neceffary you fhould pay any attention to fetting an odd number, fuch fuperftitious notions having been long abolifhed in great cities, and really if they were in fmall villages, it would be a great proof of the people's good fenfe.

I muft next caution you not to fet your ftrange hens where the others can get at them, as their wanting to fit would occafion the eggs to be broke; and if they did not want to fit, they would quarrel, which would be attended with the fame lofs. Alfo to let plenty of victuals and water be always near the hens that are fitting; and if the place where they fit is floored, provide a quantity of gravel, by which means they will be able to eat, drink, and trim themſelves at their pleaſure.

As you will take the eggs from any one of your breeding hens that wants to ſit, you muſt at the ſame time confine her, or elſe ſhe will become very troubleſome, by getting into one of the other hen's neſts, and ſo prevent her from coming to lay ; and as this in all probability may occaſion them to quarrel, you ſhould take great care to prevent it ; for very often when they begin fighting, they never run peaceably together afterwards. Beſides, there are other ill conſequences attend their quarrelling, for if the two hens that have quarrelled happened to be miſtreſſes over the others, and get the leaſt disfigured, they will be attacked by them, and if they are not parted very ſoon, it will hinder them from laying any more that ſeaſon, and ſometimes they entirely ſpoil one another. To prevent theſe diſagreeable circumſtances, when any one of them wants to ſit, and it is not agreeable to you ſhe ſhould, keep her under a crate cloſe to the ſpot where you always feed your fowls, until ſuch time as her heat for ſitting is gone off, which will not hurt her, if ſhe has a dry place to ſtand in ſhould it rain, and which you may procure her, by putting ſomething over that end of the crate where ſhe roofts; for was you to feparate them in fuch a manner as they could not fee each other, when you put them together again it would occafion a quarrel, and as I have informed you of the confequences attending fuch a thing, you fhould fpare no pains to guard againft it.

Now, Sir, fuppofe all your hens have laid their firft clutch of eggs, and gone off wanting to fit, when they begin to lay their fecond clutch, juft proceed in the fame manner as you did with the firft, only with this difference, of letting them fit on their own eggs; for by no means let them lay a third clutch before you permit them to fit, as they will be weakened by fuch a proceeding very much; neither do I think the chickens would be fo good; for it muft be underftood you made a trefpafs upon nature, in not permitting them to fit the firft time they wanted, and not only this, but the feafon would get too far advanced; it being the prevailing opinion of all good judges, that chickens bred to fight fhould be hatched in the latter end of March, or in the months of April and May. And indeed experience will fhew the neceffity there is of abiding by this obfer-vation; for if chickens are hatched in February, or the beginning of March, without the feafon is remarkably mild, it is a great chance but half of them die: befides, the trouble you will

be at in keeping them in the houfe, thofe that
do live, thrive fo flowly by reafon of their
being cramped with the cold when young, that
the other chickens hatched in April or May, by
never having any illnefs, will be much finer in
every refpect before the end of July; and as it
is not good policy to fight a match of chickens,
there is no occafion for them to be hatched fo
early, being equally as forward to fight as cocks
bred in April or May.   Nor can any perfon,
who is not well acquainted with breeding, con-
ceive the amazing difference there will be between a clutch of chickens hatched in April or
May, and one hatched in July, or Auguft, although from the fame cock and hens; for as
thofe bred in the fpring will run cocks (to make
ufe of fome phrafes made by fportfmen) high
upon leg, light flefhed, and large boned; when
thofe bred in the fummer will be quite the re-
verfe, and confequently will have to fight (if
his antagonift was bred in a proper feafon) a
much larger cock, though no heavier than
himfelf.

As one-and-twenty days is the time allotted
for a hen to hatch her chickens in, I muft ac-
quaint you, if your eggs are fet as foon as you
have a fufficient number laid, they will hatch
the twentieth day, and when the weather has
been remarkably warm, I have known them

begin hatching the nineteenth. Thefe remarks I make, that you may be attentive, and take the chickens from her as they hatch, for if you do not, and they fhould not hatch nearly toge-ther, fhe will leave off fitting fo clofe as fhe fhould do, after two or three are out of the fhell, and confequently, if fhe does, the reft muft perifh. The chickens that are taken from the hen, while the reft are hatching, muft be kept warm, which you may do, by putting them in a neft made of wool, and covered with flannel, taking care at the fame time that they are put in a place where the hen cannot hear them, for if fhe does, fhe will leave off fitting immediately, and fly to the place where they are.

If you have four hens hatch chickens in the courfe of three or four days, and each hen upon an average has not more than ten, take the chickens from one, and divide them amongft the other three, which you may do in an even-ing, after they have been fome time at rooft; and the hens they are put to, will nurfe them the morning following, in the fame manner as thofe they hatched themfelves; but fhould they not have above eight each, you may let them all be brought up by two hens, which will fave you the expence and trouble of keeping four, as two will anfwer the fame purpofe;

befides, your chickens will not have fo many enemies.

If it is dry weather, and the fun fhines, you may put your chickens out of doors the next day after they are hatched, placing your hens under crates, to prevent them rambling too far; but if the weather is cold, and the ground wet, keep them in a room, and confine the hens in the fame manner fuppofing they were out, which will occafion them to hover the chickens much oftener than if they had their liberty; but be fure there is fpace enough for the chickens to get into the crates, becaufe if they are obliged to fqueeze in, it will make them grow long bodied, as will their often going between garden rails, which they will do, if there are any near, and they cannot fly over.

I have heard many perfons declare, who could have had no experience in breeding fowls, that they did not think it neceffary that a hen fhould be confined while her chickens were young, and had juft fenfe enough to fay, that nature never defigned it; but let me tell thofe naturalifts (naturals I may call them), if a hen fhould lay a clutch of eggs fecretly in January, as it is not uncommon for young hens to lay in that month and fit upon them, confequently, if there are any chickens hatched, it muſt be in February, when if ſhe is not taken in doors, but left to range where ſhe pleaſes, I am confident that the cold northerly winds and wet weather, which are uſual at that ſeaſon of the year, will deſtroy every one of them.

Breeders differ very much with reſpect to the food that is given chickens for the firſt ten or twelve days after they are hatched, but I have always found them to thrive beſt when fed with bread and egg, mixed in the ſame manner as for young canary birds; and if it happens to be wet weather, that you are obliged to keep them in a room, give them once a-day ſome bones of raw mutton or beef to pick, for as they are deprived, by being confined, of the inſects and worms they are always picking up when ranging about in the fields, it is neceſſary they ſhould have ſome meat, and when given them in this manner, I think it is better than when it is cut for them, as it not only helps to digeſt their other food quick, but affords them exerciſe and amuſement.

It is requiſite you ſhould pay great attention to changing their water very often, for as it is given them in very ſhallow veſſels, they ſoon make it dirty, by frequently running through it, whether in a room or out of doors; beſides, when the hen is out, as she should always be placed where the sun shines, the water gets warm by there only being such a small quantity, which is very disagreeable to them, so much, that they have refused drinking it; when the instant you have given them fresh water, they have drank till they have been sick, which ought to be prevented.

When your chickens are a fortnight old, begin feeding them on barley, and let your hens have their liberty; but if you should not have the convenience of a running water, take care to place the vessels from which they are to drink the shady side of the house, and the oftener you change their water the better; likewise, I would have you feed your chickens from a place where there is gravel, which may be effected by having three or four cart loads of that soil thrown up in the same manner as a bank which separates two fields, and at feeding time scatter their barley on both sides of it, which in some measure will prevent your hens from beating each other's chickens, likewise, the early clutches from worrying the latter ones. It will also be of great service towards keeping them sound, for as they cannot help eating, in wet weather, a quantity of whatever soil their corn is scattered upon, you may be assured gravel is the wholesomest. Be sure also that they do not drink any foap-fuds, or get to any filthy places; for if they do, it engenders diftempers in them which very often turn to that fatal one the roope, a difeafe for which I have heard many remedies, but never found any fo effectual as breaking their necks; and which method every perfon fhould take, as foon as they are certain any one has that disorder. My reafon for faying when they are certain, is, that fome perfons think fowls have the roope, when they have only a matter, refembling water, running from their noftrils (which is occafioned by a cold); and though this, for certain, is the firft ftage of that diftemper, yet if you change their walk, and take care of them, they will recover without being fo much hurt as to prevent their being bred from. I have likewife known fowls which have not had their conftitution hurt, although their heads have been fwelled by a cold, that cores have been cut out from under their eyes, but this has been a fudden attack, and as fudden a recovery; for, reft yourfelf affured, if they do not lofe their running upon changing their walk, and it becomes thick and ftinks, they have got the roope, and the beft way to ufe them when that happens, I have informed you already.

C

The proper times to feed your chickens, are in the morning when you let them out *, at noon, and about an hour before you let them go to rooſt; and do not give them more at once than they can eat, that is, do not let there be victuals always upon the gravel, for if you do, they will not take that exerciſe which is neceſſary they ſhould, no more than they will if they are kept too long without feeding; and to explain the neceſſity there is for acting in this manner, is only to figure to yourſelf when you have been obliged to wait an hour or two longer for your dinner than uſual, how incapable you have found yourſelf during that time even to undertake any thing ever ſo trifling; as on the other hand, when you have been at a table where a great number of delicacies have induced you to eat more than nature required,

---

* For by no means let them have a hole to go in and out when they pleaſe, but in the day time let the door of their rooſting place ſtand open, by which if you have no other outhouſe, they will have a place of ſhelter in inclement weather; and after they are gone to rooſt lock it up, which will prevent their being diſturbed or run away with in the night by a fox, or any other vermin that prey upon poultry. Counting them every morning, if you have a great number, will enable you to find out quickly if there are any miſſing, and though you ſhould not have the good fortune to recover them, by finding it out ſo ſoon you will have it in your power to prevent any more going that way, before the loſs becomes too great.

you muſt have found yourſelf equally incapable of doing any one thing except to ſleep.

If your breeding hens have all got chickens, as it is probable they may by ſitting on their ſecond clutches of eggs, take up your cock, and put him to another walk; for by the hens being engaged, and not acccompanying him, he will get vicious and moroſe, and perhaps beat the chickens, who by being young and unable to bear his blows, will pine away and die; beſides, by his being ſent away, the hens will take care of them much longer. As ſoon as you can well diſtinguiſh the different ſpecies between the chickens, break the necks of all the pullets, except you mean to ſave any to breed from; for as you muſt break their necks when they are three or four months old, I think the trouble you will be at in keeping them ſo long, and to feed them as you do the reſt, will be more than they are worth for the table; beſides, as you bred them to have ſo much bone, the expence you have been at for barley, will buy chickens that will eat much better. But ſuppoſe your ſituation in life is ſuch that the expence is not an object worth your notice, it would be dimi-niſhing their number, which is very requiſite, as it occaſions them to thrive the faſter. In fine, it would in all probability prevent your giving any away; for was you to be viſited by any of your friends, their ſeeing ſo many pullets, might induce them to folicit one, and if they are perfons you would wifh to oblige, you cannot deny their requeft; the confequence of which will be, if ever any of thefe gentlemen fhould take part in a match againft you, your cocks will have to fight againft their own relations; which leads me to think, that gentlemen who follow this diverfion fhould live with their friends as if they would one time or another become their enemies; and although this maxim may feem rather fevere, yet I will venture to affert, was it adopted on many other occafions, it would be found a neceffary one.

When your chickens want to go to rooft, let the perches you provide for them be round and covered with woolen cloth, which will prevent their growing crooked breafted*, neither fhould it be thicker than they can gripe with eafe, as

* When a cock is called crooked breafted, it appears, when you have him in your hands, as if a piece had been cut out of his breaft bone ; and this proceeds from permitting them to rooft, while growing, upon any thing fharp. But whether this be any detriment to them in their fighting I will not pretend to determine, and can only fay, the lefs out of their proper fhape the better, for a diftorted animal of any kind feldom poffeffes the fame ftrength as if he was perfect.

that would occasion them to grow duck footed*. This last article when it happens is a great detriment to them, by reason of their not being able to stand so firm in their battle as they otherwise would do, were their claws in a proper direction. The perches likewise should be placed no higher than they can ascend with ease, moving them as they grow more able to fly, but never place them too high (that is, not higher than four or five feet, till they are three months old), for fear it should occasion them to have swelled feet; and if the perches are not taken down the hens used to roost on, they will roost there again before the chickens are able to follow them, which will render the chickens uneasy, and as they will attempt every time they go to roost, till they can accomplish their views, their wings or claws may be broke, which would entirely spoil them.

It is probable, nay I am certain you will be disagreeably perplexed on account of their fighting for master, particularly as you have so many, and I wish I could point out a method that would entirely prevent them; for very often

* Is when the short claw that should project out behind to keep the body upon an equal balance is twisted, and lies in the same direction as the claw next to it; and this is never a natural defect, but owing to letting them roost while young upon any thing flat.

C 3

they fight until they tear the skin from one another's heads half way down their necks, and when this happens, sportsmen call them peel pated, by reason that the feathers never grow afterwards where the skin has been broke; and this is so great a defect, that the opposite party may refuse to let them be weighed, alledging they have a great advantage over a cock with a fair hackle; and if they should act in this manner, after you have been at the trouble and expence of bringing them up to be cocks, (without you choose to sell them) you will be obliged to break their necks. There are also other ill consequences, if they are permitted to fight a long time, such as their getting seem eyed, cankered mouths, and to be explicit, sometimes they make one another in such a condition as obliges you to kill them directly.

Now, Sir, to prevent their fighting being attended with such disagreeable consequences, after they have begun, divide them into as many parties as you can find separate apartments, leaving the strongest upon the ground, and when these have fully established their authority over each other (which you make them do in the course of two days, by holding which you find the weakest in your hand, and buffetting him with your handkerchief while the other strikes him, and if this won't do, confine him without victuals for a few hours until he is cold, when by his being stiff and sore, and the other fresh, after a blow or two he will not attack him again) you may put down the strongest from one of the parties that are shut up, who by being kept short of food, will submit directly to run under all those that are down; and when they are so far reconciled as to permit him to run amongst them, put down the strongest from another party, which will submit in the same manner, and by pursuing this method, in the course of a few days you will be able to get them all down. When once settled they will go very peaceably together, except by accident one o them should get disfigured, which if such a thing should happen, and they do not seem to be perfectly reconciled, send him to another walk for fear of a general quarrel.

Do not permit the hens to run any longer with the chickens, than while they remain mistresses over them; but send them and the pullets you have saved to another walk; as it will be in a season of the year your brood cock can be of no service, by putting him down with the chickens, he will be as good to them as a bell weather to a flock of sheep; besides, you will save a walk, and in this manner they will run peaceably together (if you prevent any hens from coming near them), until you want the walk for breeding at again. Be sure you get good walks for those to be made cocks of, but by no means put them down at farm houses, for reasons I have taken notice of before, nor at any place where there is the least probability of their getting to other cocks, for if you do, you may be assured of having them spoiled. In short, if they are not put to good walks, where they will have plenty of good corn and clean water, you had better break their necks. When you take them to their walks, cut off their combs, &c. as close as you can; and by following these methods, your brood walk will be clear for you to begin breeding in a proper time the next season.

Having mentioned about moving your hens to another walk, I must caution you not to put them down where there are any other hens, not even dunghill ones,* for though these will not fight long enough to do your hens any injury, they will disfigure them, which is as bad, be-

---

* But as it is common for game hens to crow, if they are well fed and kept a long time without a cock, you had better caution the person where you put them (particularly if they are of those kind of people who believe in ill omens) not to break their necks; for these same people think when hens crow, it is a sure sign some person in the house will die soon, (which to prevent, the poor hens fall a sacrifice) when at the same time it is only occasioned by their being lustful.

cauſe it will ſet them a fighting among themſelves; and if you mean to breed from them
the next ſeaſon, it would certainly be better to
let them run without a cock ; for if they do not
lay after they have began to moult, till the
clutch of eggs you would wiſh to ſet, you will
not be certain to the father of your chickens.

I think it requiſite you ſhould know the
goodneſs of thoſe already bred before you breed
another whole ſeaſon from the ſame cock and
hens, but do not cut them out as ſome perſons
do, who think if they die game they muſt be
good ones; for inſtance, ſome gentleman's
cocks, although very good game, have been
beat very eaſy only by half bred cocks, that
have been good ſtrikers; whereas if they had
made as good uſe of their heels as their antago-
niſts, they would eaſily have made them run
away. But to be ingenuous, the method I
would have you follow to find out their goodneſs,
is to chooſe three or four that are ſhorteſt upon
leg (becauſe they are the fitteſt to fight when
ſtags) from thoſe that were hatched in the early
part of the ſeaſon, and if you are concerned in
a match about February or March, have them
weighed in; but ſuppoſing you ſhould not have
any thing to do with a match, lend them where
you are ſure they will be well looked after, and
by ſtaking the battle money they fight for, you

may have them weighed to fight in the main, which I would have you do; and as you would not have lent them without its being a creditable match, they consequently will have to fight against good cocks. If you lend four, it is probable three may fight; but there is great odds that one does, and about an equal chance that two does; but let us suppose three fight, I think you would be to blame to back them, and indeed it would be judgment for you to lay against them to the amount of the battle money, for although your stags may be much better than the cocks they fight against, yet if it should be a long battle, the cocks must win without a mere chance; which good sportsmen never will trust to. I think it also requisite, you should inform yourself, if you can, whose cocks your stags fight against, and what character they bear, for by so doing, you will be a better judge what your stags are able to do; likewise, pay a strict attention to their manner of fighting, for if they keep the battle upon an equal poise against good cocks, and only seem to be beat by age, do not be out of humour, and break the necks of those at their walks, as you may expect great things from them when cocks. Supposing they should behave in this manner, breed from the same cock and hens again the next season, and should they win the odd battle when cocks, be very careful of your brood cock; for if you are, and by keeping him from the hens during the latter part of the feafon, you may breed from him feven or eight years, as a cock that will get good chickens, being a very valuable acquifition to a breeder.

But I dó not mean, when I fay you may breed from your cock fo many feafons, that it fhould always be from the fame hens, neither do I think there is any occafion to crofs them every feafon, for if they are good, be contented, (and do not let every cock you fee fight a good battle, entice you to breed from him) for by putting your young hens to your old cock, and a young cock to your old hens, you may keep them in their full vigour at leaft four years. But never breed from ftags nor pullets with your old ones, as no fowls can ever be poffeffed of every neceffary requifite to breed from, until they have moulted twice, and when you do crofs your breed, be very careful what fort you do it with, and the nearer the colour of your own the better, as the produce will run more regular in feather.

Now, Sir, permit me to recommend you to tranfact the bufinefs relative to trying your ftags, without mentioning it even to the perfon that feeds them, which you may effect by cutting off the points of your ftags heels when you take them from their walks, and fending them as cocks: but if he fhould have fome fufpicion they are ftags (as it is probable he will, if he underftands his bufinefs) and afks you, do not inform him, neither tell him they are your own breeding, or that they are all of one fort; by which means, whether they are good or bad, no perfon will be acquainted with it; for if they fhould turn out to be of the firft rate, and you have told the feeder they are your own, and that you have a great many brothers, he tells his helpers, and they their companions, by which means, when your cocks come to fight the next year, you will not be able to get a bet, without laying fix to four, and fuppofing you lay an equal fum upon every battle, if your cocks do win three out of five in one day's fighting you will be but juft even in your bets; but if they fhould lofe three out of five the next day, and you kept laying guineas, you would be ten lofer.

I think this is fufficient to fhew you, how neceffary it is to act with fecrecy. And to prevent any one from knowing that your cocks are all of one fort, when you mark your chickens, do it two or three different ways, but do not truft to your memory on this occafion, let it be ever fo good, for by having two or three forts, each marked in a different manner, may create confufion, if not inferted in a book.

Before I conclude this short Treatise, it will be requisite to make some necessary remarks, to be attended to by any gentleman that is going to fight a match. In fine, when a gentleman has an intention of fighting a match, no matter whether for one day or a week, before he comes to an agreement, he should visit all his walks, to see if his cocks are safe and in a condition fit to be taken up; if they are, the next thing to be considered is to secure a feeder, one whose cocks he has known to fight well during the course of many matches, and not by his only having the name of a good feeder, for many are called by that name who have little pretensions to it; and if they have had the good fortune to win a match or two, it has not been owing so much to their good feeding, as to the excellent string of cocks that have been sent in by the gentlemen who employed them. Likewise to secure a good setter-to, one whom you have seen often and know to be clever, for it is the same with this art as I have observed concerning feeding, many pretending to be adepts in it, who do not know when a cock wants rest; or when he should be made to fight. It must be understood, the winning of a match chiefly depends upon these two persons, for I have known a good feeder and a good setter-to, win a match with an indifferent string of cocks, against a bad feeder and setter-to with an ex-

D

cellent one; and as there are generally two who have more merit than any that pretend to this art, the perſon who ſecures them in his intereſt will conſequently have a great advantage over his adverſary.

ORDERS AND RULES

FOR

COCKING,

As abided by at the

COCKPIT-ROYAL.

ON the weighing morning, that perſon whoſe chance is to weigh laſt, is to ſet his cocks and number his pens, both main and byes, and leave the key of the pens upon the weighing table, (or the other party, if he pleaſes, may put a lock on the door) before any cock is put into the ſcale, and after the firſt pack of cocks are weighed, a perſon appointed by him that weighed firſt, ſhall go into the other pens to ſee that no other cocks are weighed but what are ſo ſet and numbered, provided they are

within the articles of weight that the match
specify; if not, to take the following cock or
cocks, until the whole number of main and bye
cocks are weighed through. And after they
are all weighed, you are to proceed as soon as
possible to match them, beginning at the least
weight first, and so on; and equal weights or
nearest weights to be separated, provided by
that separation a greater number of battles can
be made, and not otherwise; and all blanks,
that is, choice of cocks, are to be filled up on
the weighing day, and the battles divided and
struck off for each day's play, as agreed on, and
the cocks that weigh the least are to fight the
first day, and so upwards.

At the same time agreed on by both parties
to begin fighting, the cocks that are to fight
the first battle are brought upon the pit by the
feeders, or their helpers; and after being ex-
amined, to see they answer the marks and colours specified in the match-bill, they are given
to the setters-to, who, after chopping them in
hand, give them to the gentlemen who are called masters of the match (who always fit opposite to each other) when they turn them
down upon the mat; and the setters-to are not
to touch them, except they either hang in the
mat, in each other, or get close to the edge of
the pit, until they leave off fighting, while a
person can tell forty.

When both cocks leave off fighting, until one of the fetters-to, or a perfon appointed for telling the law, can tell forty gradually, then the fetters-to are to make the neareft way to their cocks, and as foon as they have taken them up, to carry them into the middle of the pit, and immediately deliver them on their legs beak to beak, and not touch them any more until they have refufed fighting, fo long as the teller of the law can tell ten, without they are on their backs, or hung in each other, or in the mat; then they are to fet to again in the fame manner as before, and continue it till one cock refufes fighting ten feveral times, one after another, when it is that cock's battle that fought within the law.

But it fometimes happens that both cocks refufe fighting while the law is telling; when this happens, a frefh cock is to be hovelled, and brought upon the mat as foon as poffible, and the fetters to are to tofs up, which cock is to be fet to firft, and he that gets the chance is to choofe, Then the other which is to be fet to laft, muft be taken up, but not carried off the pit; then fetting the hovelled cock down to the other five feparate times, telling ten between each fetting to, and then the fame to the other cock; and if one fights and the other refufes, it is a battle to the fighting cock; but if both fight, or both refuse, it is a drawn battle. The reason of setting-to five times to each cock, is, that ten times setting-to being the long law, so on their both refusing, the law is to be equally divided between them, as they are both entitled to it alike.

Another way of deciding a battle is, if any person offers to lay ten pounds to a crown (that is, if he is a person thought capable of laying it if he loses, or one who stakes his money on the mat) and no person takes it until the law teller tells forty, and calls out three separate times, "Will any one take it?" an if no one does, it is the cock's battle the odds are laid on, and the setters-to are not to touch the cocks during the time the forty is taking, without either cock is hung in the mat, or on his back, or hung together.

If a cock should die before the long law is told out, although he fought in the law, and the other did not, he loses his battle, for sure there cannot be a better rule for a cock winning his battle than killing his adversary, in the limited time he is entitled to by cock laws.

There are often disputes with the setters-to, as also with the spectators, that is, in setting-to in the long law, for often both cocks refuse fighting until four or five, or more or lefs times, are told; then they begin telling from that cock's fighting, and counting but once refufed, but they fhould continue their number on, until one cock has refufed ten times; for when the law is begun to be told, it is for both cocks; for if one cock fights within the long law, and the other not, it is a battle to the cock that fought, counting from the firft fetting-to.

All difputes about bets, or the battle being won or loft, ought to be decided by the fpectators, for if the bets are not paid, nor the battles fettled according to judgment then given, it will be a good evidence in law if an action is brought for the recovery of fuch bets. The crowning and mantling of a cock, or fighting at the fetter-to's hand before he is put to the other cock, or breaking from his antagonift, is allowed no fight.

ARTICLES

ARTICLES

For a

COCK MATCH,

As made Use of at the

COCK-PIT ROYAL,

WESTMINSTER.

————————————

ARTICLES of agreement made the ː.... day of ..... One thousand seven hundred and .... between ....
....
....
....
First, the said parties have agreed, that each of them shall produce, shew, and weigh, at the ....
....
....
on the ...... day of .... beginning at the hour of .... in the morning, ... cocks, none to be less than three pounds six ounces, nor more than four pounds eight ounces, and as many of each parties cocks that come within one ounce of each other shall fight for .... a battle, that is, ... each cock; in as equal

divifions as the battles can be divided into fix pits, or days play at the cock-pit before mentioned; and the parties cocks that win the greateft number of battles, matched out of the number before fpecified, fhall be entitled to the fum of . . . . odd battle money, and the fum to be ftaked into the hands of Mr. . . . . before any cocks are pitted, by both parties. And we further agree, to produce, fhew, and weigh, on the faid weighing days . . . . . cocks for bye battles, fubject to the fame weight as the cocks that fight in the main, and thefe to be added to the number of main cocks unmatched, and as many of them as come within one ounce of each other, fhall fight for . . . . a battle; the number of cocks fo matched, to be equally divided as will permit of, and added to each day's play with the main cocks, and it is alfo agreed, that the balance of the battle money fhall be paid at the end of each day's play. It is alfo further agreed, for the cocks to fight in filver fpurs, and with fair hackles, and to be fubject to all the ufual rules of cock-fighting as practifed at the Cock-Pit Royal, Weftminfter, and the profits arifing from the fpectators, to be equally divided between both parties, after all charges are paid that ufually happen on thofe occafions. Witnefs our hands the . . . . . . day of 17

Witnefs . . . .

KET

K E Y

TO A

M A T C H   B I L L

A. B's Cocks.	C. D's Cocks.
Lb. Oz.	
3 6	
1	
2	
3	
————	
7	
1	
2	
3	
————	
8	
1	
2	
3	
————	
9	
1	
2	
3	
————	
10	
1	
2	
3	
————	
11	
1	
2	
3	

A. B's Cocks.   C, D's Cocks.

Lb.	Oz.	
3	12	
	1	
	2	
	3	
	13	
	1	
	2	
	3	
	14	
	1	
	2	
	3	
	15	
	1	
	2	
	3	
4	0	
	0	
	1	
	2	
	3	
	1	
	1	
	2	
	3	
	2	
	1	
	2	
	3	

A. B's Cocks.		C. D's Cocks,
Lb.	Oz.	
4	3	
	1	
	2	
	3	
	—	
	4	
	1	
	2	
	3	
	—	
	5	
	1	
	2	
	3	
	—	
	6	
	1	
	2	
	3	
	—	
	7	
	1	
	2	
	3	
	—	
	8	

N. B. Place the number the cock is weighed in each column, in a parallel line againſt this weight.

CALCULATIONS

FOR

COCKING.

Battles		Odds	
3 out of 4	is	$2\frac{1}{5}$	to 1
4 out of 5	is	$4\frac{1}{3}$	to 1
4 out of 6	is	$1\frac{10}{11}$	to 1
5 out of 6	is	$8\frac{1}{7}$	to 1
5 out of 7	is	$3\frac{12}{29}$	to 1
6 out of 7	is	15	to 1
5 out of 8	is	$1\frac{70}{93}$	to 1
6 out of 8	is	$5\frac{34}{37}$	to 1
7 out of 8	is	$27\frac{4}{9}$	to 1
6 out of 9	is	$2\frac{122}{130}$	to 1
7 out of 9	is	$10\frac{6}{46}$	to 1
8 out of 9	is	$50\frac{1}{2}$	to 1
6 out of 10	is	$1\frac{252}{386}$	to 1
7 out of 10	is	$4\frac{144}{176}$	to 1
8 out of 10	is	$17\frac{16}{56}$	to 1
9 out of 10	is	$92\frac{1}{11}$	to 1
7 out of 11	is	$2\frac{362}{562}$	to 1

Battles		Odds	
8 out of 11	is	$7 \frac{192}{232}$	to 1
9 out of 11	is	$29 \frac{38}{67}$	to 1
10 out of 11	is	$169 \frac{8}{12}$	to 1
7 out of 12	is	$1 \frac{924}{1586}$	to 1
8 out of 12	is	$4 \frac{126}{704}$	to 1
9 out of 12	is	$12 \frac{209}{299}$	to 1
10 out of 12	is	$50 \frac{67}{79}$	to 1
11 out of 12	is	$314 \frac{1}{13}$	to 1
8 out of 13	is	$2 \frac{263}{595}$	to 1
9 out of 13	is	$6 \frac{541}{1093}$	to 1
10 out of 13	is	$20 \frac{127}{189}$	to 1
11 out of 13	is	$88 \frac{1}{23}$	to 1
12 out of 13	is	$584 \frac{1}{7}$	to 1
8 out of 14	is	$1 \frac{608}{1519}$	to 1
9 out of 14	is	$3 \frac{2442}{3473}$	to 1
10 out of 14	is	$10 \frac{203}{1471}$	to 1
11 out of 14	is	$33 \frac{202}{235}$	to 1
12 out of 14	is	$153 \frac{30}{103}$	to 1
13 out of 14	is	$1091 \frac{4}{15}$	to 1
9 out of 15	is	$2 \frac{2921}{9949}$	to 1
10 out of 15	is	$5 \frac{3104}{4044}$	to 1
11 out of 15	is	$15 \frac{1712}{1941}$	to 1
12 out of 15	is	$55 \frac{512}{576}$	to 1
13 out of 15	is	$269 \frac{98}{121}$	to 1
14 out of 15	is	2047	to 1
9 out of 16	is	$1 \frac{12870}{26333}$	to 1
10 out of 16	is	$3 \frac{5964}{14993}$	to 1
11 out of 16	is	$8 \frac{3571}{6885}$	to 1
12 out of 16	is	$25 \frac{n4}{2571}$	to 1
13 out of 16	is	$93 \frac{18}{697}$	to 1

E

Battles	is	Odds	to 1
14 out of 16	is	$477 \frac{50}{137}$	to 1
15 out of 16	is	$3854 \frac{1}{17}$	to 1
10 out of 17	is	$1 \frac{3602}{20613}$	to 1
11 out of 17	is	$5 \frac{202}{10889}$	to 1
12 out of 17	is	$12 \frac{4423}{4701}$	to 1
13 out of 17	is	$39 \frac{1256}{1607}$	to 1
14 out of 17	is	$156 \frac{67}{417}$	to 1
15 out of 17	is	$850 \frac{9}{77}$	to 1
16 out of 17	is	$7280 \frac{7}{9}$	to 1
10 out of 18	is	$1 \frac{48620}{107662}$	to 1
11 out of 18	is	$3 \frac{10128}{53004}$	to 1
12 out of 18	is	$7 \frac{12704}{31180}$	to 1
13 out of 18	is	$19 \frac{9824}{12616}$	to 1
14 out of 18	is	$63 \frac{3072}{4048}$	to 1
15 out of 18	is	$264 \frac{324}{988}$	to 1
16 out of 18	is	$1523 \frac{16}{172}$	to 1
17 out of 18	is	$13796 \frac{1}{19}$	to 1
11 out of 19	is	$2 \frac{57495}{84883}$	to 1
12 out of 19	is	$4 \frac{6671}{11773}$	to 1
13 out of 19	is	$10 \frac{10633}{10949}$	to 1
14 out of 19	is	$30 \frac{938}{2083}$	to 1
15 out of 19	is	$103 \frac{136}{1259}$	to 1
16 out of 19	is	$450 \frac{141}{145}$	to 1
17 out of 19	is	$2743 \frac{184}{191}$	to 1
18 out of 19	is	$26213 \frac{3}{5}$	to 1
11 out of 20	is	$1 \frac{184756}{431910}$	to 1
12 out of 20	is	$2 \frac{256726}{263950}$	to 1
13 out of 20	is	$6 \frac{82726}{137980}$	to 1
14 out of 20	is	$16 \frac{20756}{60460}$	to 1
15 out of 20	is	$47 \frac{6976}{21700}$	to 1

Battles		Odds
16 out of 20	is	$168 \frac{1452}{6196}$ to 1
17 out of 20	is	$775 \frac{200}{1351}$ to 1
18 out of 20	is	$4968 \frac{117}{211}$ to 1
19 out of 20	is	$49931 \frac{5}{21}$ to 1

N. B. The foregoing Calculations suppose even money on each battle.

A TABLE

Shewing the Odds for and against one Side winning a certain number of Battles, when there is even money on each Battle.

Battles		Odds
4	One side wins 3 out of 4 is	11 to 5
5	Neither wins 4 out of 5 is	5 to 10
6	One side wins 4 out of 6 is	11 to 5
	Neither wins 5 out of 6 is	25 to 7
7	Neither wins 5 out of 7 is	35 to 29
8	Neither wins 6 out of 8 is	91 to 37
9	One side wins 6 out of 9 is	65 to 63
	Neither wins 7 out of 9 is	105 to 23
10	Neither wins 7 out of 10 is	21 to 11
11	One side wins 7 out of 11 is	281 to 231
	Neither wins 8 out of 11 is	787 to 232
12	One side wins 7 out of 12 is	793 to 231

Battles		Odds
	Neither wins 8 out of 12 is	602 to 397
13	One side wins 8 out of 13 is	595 to 429
	Neither wins 9 out of 13 is	3003 to 1093
14	One side wins 9 out of 14 is	4473 to 3719
15	One side wins 9 out of 15 is	9949 to 1335
	Neither wins 10 out of 15 is	11435 to 4954
16	One side wins 9 out of 16 is	26333 to 6435
	Neither wins 13 out of 16 is	17875 to 14893
17	One side wins 10 out of 17 is	20613 to 12158
	Neith. w. 11 out of 17 is	136136 to 126008
20	One s. w. 12 out of 20 is	131725 to 130169

The foregoing Table is so plain, that it needs no explanation.

When there are five battles to fight, it is an equal wager that one side wins three battles running.

And when six battles, then it is five to three that one side wins three battles running.

It is $3\frac{2}{5}$ to 1, you do not win two battles running, when each battle is six to five against you; and $2\frac{13}{36}$ to 1 you do not, when each battle is six to five for you, near fifty shillings to a guinea.

It is $4\frac{1}{16}$ to 1, you do not win two battles running, when each battle is five to four againſt you ; and $2\frac{6}{25}$ to 1, when each battle is five to four for you.

It is $5\frac{1}{4}$ to 1, you do not win two battles running, when each battle is ſix to four againſt you ;· and $1\frac{7}{9}$ to 1 you do not, when each battle is ſix to four for you.

It is 8 to 1 you do not win two battles running, when each battle is two to one againſt you ;· and five to four you do not, when the odds in each battle is two to one for you.

Suppoſing each battle ſix to five for you, it is 94176 to 66875 (above ſeven to five) you win the odd battle out of five ; but it is 120875 to 40176 (above three to one) you do not win four battles out of five; and almoſt twenty to one you do not win all five ; but it is above fifty to one you do not loſe all five, and near $6\frac{4}{11}$ to 1 you do not loſe four out of the five. And if each battle be five to four for you, it is 35625 to 23424 (above ſix to four) you win the odd battle out of the five, and $17\frac{2792}{3125}$ to 1 you do not win all the five ; but it is $6\frac{7081}{7424}$ to 1 you do not loſe four out of the five, and $56\frac{681}{1024}$ to 1 you do not loſe all five.

When there are only two battles to fight, it is $5\frac{1}{4}$ to 1 you do not win both, when the odds is six to four against you; and $1\frac{7}{9}$ to 1 you do not, when each battle is six to four for you.

When the odds are 2 to 1 for you, it is five to four you do not win two battles running; and eight to one you do not lose both.

When there are four battles to fight, and the odds are 2 to 1 for you, then it is 65 to 16, or $4\frac{1}{16}$ to 1 you do not win all four; but it is 80 to 1 you do not lose all.

And if the odds are 2 to 1 for you, then it will be 131 to 132 that you do not win four out of the five, and 211 to 32, or $6\frac{19}{32}$ to 1 you do not win all five; but it is 232 to 1 you do not lose four out of the five; and 242 to 1 you do not lose all five; and likewise it is 1248 to 939 you do not win five out of seven, and 1911 to 276 you do not six out of seven, and 2059 to 128 or $16\frac{11}{128}$ to 1 you do not win all seven; but it is 2078 to 109 you do not lose five out of seven; and 2172 to 15, or $144\frac{4}{5}$ to 1 you do not lose six, and 2186 to 1, not all 7.

The odds of a match in which there are even battles, and one side is three, four, or any other number of battles ahead, it is double the odds you do not tie the match, more the odds you do not win it, lefs one to two.

EXAMPLE.

Suppofe in a match of thirty battles, one fide was three ahead, and but feven battles to fight, then the other muft win five out of the feven to tie, and fix out of feven to win the match: look in the Table, and you will find it is $3\frac{12}{29}$ to 1, not 5, and 15 to 1, not 6 out of 7.   The double of $3\frac{12}{29}$ is $6\frac{24}{29}$ more, 15 is $21\frac{24}{29}$ lefs, 1 is $20\frac{24}{29}$ to 2 in the odds of fuch a match.

Suppofe nine battles to fight, and one fide is five battles ahead, then the other fide muft win feven out of nine to fave, and eight out of nine to win, therefore the odds will be $69\frac{4}{5}$ to 1.

ODDS IN THE MAIN OF

ODDS IN EACH BATTLE.	THREE BATTLES.	FIVE BATTLES.	SEVEN BATTLES.
2 to 1	is 2 $\frac{6}{7}$ to 1	is 3 $\frac{39}{61}$ to 1	is 4 $\frac{292}{379}$ to 1
3 to 2	is 1 $\frac{37}{44}$ to 1	is 2 $\frac{149}{592}$ to 1	is 2 $\frac{10205}{22640}$ to 1
3 to 1	is 5 $\frac{2}{5}$ to 1	is 8 $\frac{35}{53}$ to 1	is 13 $\frac{50}{289}$ to 1
5 to 4	is 1 $\frac{121}{304}$ to 1	is 1 $\frac{12199}{23426}$ to 1	is 1 $\frac{1148281}{1817344}$ to 1
5 to 3	is 2 $\frac{13}{81}$ to 1	is 2 $\frac{2857}{4509}$ to 1	is 3 $\frac{14635}{127413}$ to 1
6 to 5	is 1 $\frac{181}{575}$ to 1	is 1 $\frac{20301}{65875}$ to 1	is 1 $\frac{3843421}{7821375}$ to 1
7 to 6	is 1 $\frac{253}{972}$ to 1	is 1 $\frac{53341}{151976}$ to 1	is 1 $\frac{104963890}{261266064}$ to 1
7 to 5	is 1 $\frac{214}{325}$ to 1	is 1 $\frac{38166}{43125}$ to 1	is 2 $\frac{2855777}{2890875}$ to 1
7 to 4	is 2 $\frac{131}{400}$ to 1	is 2 $\frac{37100}{41344}$ to 1	is 3 $\frac{2110915}{4344064}$ to 1
8 to 6	is 1 $\frac{73}{135}$ to 1	is 1 $\frac{4441}{6183}$ to 1	is 1 $\frac{252169}{285687}$ to 1

SUPPOSE EVEN BETS ON BOTH SIDES, THEN ONE WINS

3 out of 4 is	5	to	3,	or	$1\frac{2}{3}$ to 1
6 out of 9 is	65	to	63,	or	$1\frac{2}{63}$ to 1
7 out of 11 is	231	to	181,	or	$1\frac{50}{181}$ to 1
8 out of 13 is	2380	to	1716,	or	$1\frac{664}{1716}$ to 1
9 out of 15 is	9949	to	6435,	or	$1\frac{3514}{6435}$ to 1
10 out of 17 is	20613	to	12155,	or	$1\frac{8458}{12155}$ to 1
not 11 is	21879	to	10889,	or	$2\frac{101}{10889}$ to 1
11 out of 19 is	84883	to	46189,	or	$1\frac{39694}{46189}$ to 1
not 12 is	20995	to	11773,	or	$1\frac{9222}{11773}$ to 1
12 out of 21 is	173965	to	88179,	or	$1\frac{85786}{88179}$ to 1
not 13 is	323323	to	200965,	or	$1\frac{122358}{200965}$ to 1
13 out of 23 is	2842226	to	1352078,	or	$2\frac{69035}{676039}$ to 1
not 14 is	156009	to	106135,	or	$1\frac{49874}{106135}$ to 1

A TABLE

Shewing the odds against each side winning two battles running.

THE STRONG SIDE.								ODDS IN EACH.			THE WEAK SIDE.							
£.	s.	d.			£.	s.	d.				£.	s.	d.			£.	s.	d.
o	8	3		to	o	4	o	8	to	6	o	17	9¼	⅓	to	o	4	o
o	7	9	12/49	to	o	4	o	7	to	5	o	19	o¼	23/29	to	o	4	o
o	7	1¼	⅓	to	o	4	o	6	to	4	1	1	o		to	o	4	o
o	6	6¾		to	o	4	o	8	to	5	1	3	o¼	23/25	to	o	4	o
o	6	2¾	13/25	to	o	4	o	5	to	3	1	4	5¼	⅕	to	o	4	o
o	5	10½	6/49	to	o	4	o	7	to	4	1	6	3		to	o	4	o
o	5	8	43/81	to	o	4	o	9	to	5	1	7	4¼	7/25	to	o	4	o
o	5	o		to	o	4	o	2	to	1	1	12	o		to	o	4	o

The Use of the foregoing Table.

Suppose a match between Kent and Middlesex, and the odds are six to five Middlesex against Kent each battle; it will be 9s. 5d.$\frac{1}{4}$ and $\frac{1}{3}$ of a farthing, to 4s. that Middlesex does not win the next two battles: and it is 15s. 4d.$\frac{1}{4}$ and $\frac{7}{25}$ of a farthing to 4s. that Kent does not win the next two battles.

If the bets are eight to seven, each battle in favour of Middlesex, then it is 10s. and $\frac{3}{4}$ to 4s. that Middlesex does not win the two next battles; and 14s. 4d.$\frac{1}{4}$ and $\frac{31}{49}$ to 4s. Kent does not win the next two battles.

———

When thirty battles is in a match it is 918624304 to 155117520 not a drawn match, almost 6 to 1.

And 4 $\frac{124796}{184756}$ to 1   when 20 battles.
And 4 $\frac{19444}{48620}$ to 1   when 18 battles.
And 4 $\frac{1186}{12876}$ to 1   when 16 battles.
And 3 $\frac{2636}{3432}$ to 1   when 14 battles.
And 3 $\frac{400}{924}$ to 1   when 12 battles.
And 3 $\frac{16}{252}$ to 1   when 10 battles.
And 2 $\frac{46}{70}$ to 1   when 8 battles.
And 2 $\frac{1}{3}$ to 1   when 6 battles.
And 1 $\frac{2}{3}$ to 1   when 4 battles.

These Calculations suppose even money on each battle.

THE END.